LOST AND FOUND

DAWN PURNEY

ASTONISHING HEADLINES

Attacked	Missing
Captured	Shot Down
Condemned	Stowed Away
Kidnapped	Stranded at Sea
Lost and Found	Trapped

Development: Kent Publishing Services, Inc.
Design and Production: Signature Design Group, Inc.

SADDLEBACK EDUCATIONAL PUBLISHING
Three Watson
Irvine, CA 92618-2767
Website: www.sdlback.com

Photo Credits: cover, page 24, Rodney Turner, KRT; page 16 (top), page 17, Seamas Culligan, Zuma Press; page 29, Barry Batchelor, PA Photos; page 41, Matt Campbell, Agence France Presse; page 49, Mario Ruiz, Zuma Press

ISBN-13: 978-1-56254-822-3
ISBN-10: 1-56254-822-0
eBook: 978-1-60291-008-9

Printed in the United States of America

12 11 10 09 08 9 8 7 6 5 4

TABLE OF CONTENTS

Introduction

Explore the mysteries behind the famous stories of things lost and found.

The city of Pompeii in Italy had long been forgotten when a farmer found a piece of it under his field. Although the city was "lost" long ago, people still find pieces of the buildings, the cookware, and sometimes, even human remains. As each piece is found, the world learns a little more about the past.

We know everything there is to know about famous pilot, Amelia Earhart. Everything, that is, except why and where her plane went down on her last flight. Modern searchers have found some clues. But so far, no one knows for sure what happened to this famous pilot.

When Adriana Scott visited another college, many people greeted her as if they knew her. Imagine her surprise when she later met her identical twin. Neither girl knew she had a sister, let alone an identical twin sister!

Modern technology brought a dog back to its owner. After three years of wandering, a woman found Tuffy 32 miles from home. All it took was a scanner to tell where Tuffy belonged!

The story of the HMS *Beagle* might sound like another dog story, but it is not. The *Beagle* was the ship a famous scientist traveled in. The *Beagle* was soon forgotten. One day, people started looking for the *Beagle*. They might have found it. But it was not floating in water, it was buried in mud.

As technology develops, people continue the search for their lost items. What would you like to find?

Pompeii – A Lost and Found City
DATAFILE

TIMELINE

August 79 C.E.

Mount Vesuvius erupts. The city of Pompeii is buried under 19 to 20 feet of ash.

1748

The city of Pompeii is found.

Where is Pompeii?

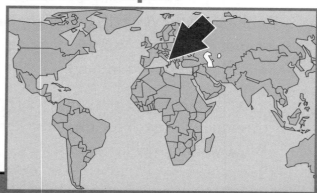

KEY TERMS

C.E. - Common Era; the years from 1 to the present

erupt - to explode violently

amphitheater - an open, oval arena with seats around it

artifact - a man-made object from a period in the past

DID YOU KNOW?

The 79 C.E. eruption of Vesuvius was the first ever to be described in detail. Pliny the Younger watched the eruption from 18 miles away. His uncle, Pliny the Elder, led a rescue team to save the people of Pompeii. Pliny the Younger wrote about the eruption in two letters that were found hundreds of years later.

Chapter One:
Pompeii – A Lost and Found City

The Volcano Destroys a City

How does one lose an entire city? It is not as hard as it sounds! A volcano covered a city in 23 feet of ash. No one could live there anymore. Over time, people forgot the covered city altogether. The story of Pompeii's disappearance begins almost 2,000 years ago, in 79 C.E.

Mount Vesuvius was a fiery volcano. It had erupted before; it would erupt again. But this time, Mount Vesuvius destroyed an entire city and all the land around it. Unlike other eruptions before, people in the area had only one day's warning about the eruption.

Hot ash from the volcano started fires in Pompeii. A rescue team tried to get to the city by boat. By the time they came close, the volcano was erupting. Sadly, most of the rescue team also died.

The eruption itself is not what killed the people of Pompeii. It was the huge rocks and burning ash that rained down on the city. Poisonous gases made people choke and gasp for air. Soon the city was completely covered in ash.

Many survivors moved away. Some moved closer to other family members. Some just moved to get away from the sad memories. Over time, no one was left who remembered the city of Pompeii.

The Discovery

In 1734, a farmer dug a well in his field. As he dug, he discovered valuable pieces of marble. He thought he could sell them. A shopkeeper bought the marble for a very good price.

In turn, a local prince bought the marble. He asked the shopkeeper where he could get more. Later, the prince bought the land from the farmer. The prince began to dig. He started to uncover an entire building, but he never finished the job.

Later, another ruler hired many people to uncover the building. They did not know what they had found, but they knew it was something interesting. In time, the searchers found a statue with the word *Pompeii* on it. It was the name of a city they had only heard about. They were the first people to see the city for more than 1,500 years!

Uncovered

The men also found what looked like a body. The ash had surrounded the body and then hardened. The body decayed over time, leaving the ash-rock mold in its place. As they found more "bodies," people were able to learn about life long ago. They even found a dog's body outside one of the houses.

Besides people and animals, many buildings, homes, and shops in the city were uncovered. The ash even kept the paint colors from fading during all that time.

The men also found a huge amphitheater. There were seats for 10,000 people. It is one of many buildings that has been completely uncovered and cleaned up.

Today

Mount Vesuvius has erupted more than 30 times since it buried Pompeii. The last eruption was more than 60 years ago. Although Mount Vesuvius has not erupted lately, it is still active. In fact, it is the only active volcano on mainland Europe. Scientists warn that any active volcano could erupt again with little or no warning.

Visitors can travel to the area today. Two small villages nearby that were also buried, now have been rebuilt into small cities. No one lives in Pompeii. But it is a popular tourist attraction.

Pompeii in the Modern World

Parts of our own culture have been influenced by Pompeii. For example, artists today use a shade called Pompeii red after the bright red color found on the city murals.

Ruins of the ancient city Pompeii

Also, the word *lava* comes from Italy. The Italian word *lava* means "a stream caused suddenly by rain." People watching Vesuvius erupt saw the molten rock flowing down the mountain. They did not know what to call it, so they used the word *lava*.

The discovery of Pompeii has sparked interest in history and historical objects. Early searchers took objects from a Pompeii home. They showed those objects to many people. Soon, others wanted to learn more about the past.

Archaeology

Archaeology is the study of past human life and culture from the artifacts that remain. People interested in studying the past through its artifacts are called archaeologists. They find and examine objects from the past, such as tools, buildings, graves, and pottery.

These things are especially useful if the people left no written record of their lives.

Archaeologists find useful objects to study painted on the walls of caves, hidden in old buildings, and buried in the ground. Sometimes they dig for these artifacts. They must be very careful not to break or lose any part of the item. After all, there may not be another one left in the whole world!

People have learned much about this ancient culture from the artifacts archaeologists found inside Pompeii. Even now, archaeologists dig up and study objects from the ancient city.

Rediscovering Pompeii

Archaeologists have uncovered much of Pompeii, including painted murals like this one.

Sadly, people in Pompeii were buried alive by ash and mud. The shape of this body was preserved when plaster was poured into the ash-rock mold that was left after the body decayed.

*This amphitheater in Pompeii seated
10,000 people.*

Amelia Earhart – A Modern Mystery

DATAFILE

TIMELINE

January 1935

Amelia Earhart is first to fly alone across the Pacific Ocean.

July 1937

Earhart disappears while trying to be first to fly around the equator.

Where is New Guinea?

19

Chapter Two:
Amelia Earhart –
A Modern Mystery

Amelia Earhart is known for her independent spirit. She learned to pilot a plane at a time when women rarely worked outside the home. She had already made a name for herself by the time she got married. In fact, her name was so famous, Amelia Earhart did not change her name to Putnam, her husband's name, when she married George Putnam in 1931.

Setting Records

The airplane was invented in 1903. However, most people did not use planes as transportation. At that time, pilots were true pioneers. Early pilots helped develop the art of flying. They tested their planes' limits. They tested their own limits. The science of flying an aircraft, called *aviation*, grew and developed.

Amelia Earhart was a pioneer in aviation. She helped start a club for the few women pilots in America. It was called The Ninety-Nines, and it still exists today. Earhart was the first woman to fly over the Atlantic Ocean. She set records for how high, how fast, and how far anyone had flown before.

Several of Earhart's flights were solo flights that took more than 12 hours. A solo flight is one in which the pilot is alone in the cockpit. Other times she flew with others who navigated or co-piloted. Earhart was proud of her records. She also gave credit to those who helped her.

One Last Trip

The last trip Amelia Earhart made resulted in one of the biggest mysteries of the twentieth century. Earhart said: "[I have] about one more good flight in my system." So, she decided to set one more record.

Earhart wanted to be the first person to fly around the world at the equator. The equator is almost 25,000 miles around. Others had flown around the world, but they had flown at the Arctic Circle, which is not as wide.

The trip would be very difficult. Earhart asked Fred Noonan to be her navigator. Together they planned where to stop, rest, and refuel. Their trip would really be 29,000 miles long because they needed to find places where they could land safely and buy gas.

On June 1, 1937, the pair left from Miami, Florida. They headed east. It took more than a month for Earhart and Noonan to fly most of the way around the world. They stopped in New Guinea. They got rid of their extra cargo and made room for extra fuel.

Earhart's next stop would be the toughest yet. The island they were aiming for was very small. Four U.S. Coast Guard ships turned on all their lights and sailed to places along the way so Earhart could see which way to fly. One ship kept in contact with Earhart by radio.

Without a Trace

Halfway across the Pacific Ocean, the Coast Guard lost radio contact with Earhart. The plane never showed up at the next place they had planned to stop.

Amelia Earhart was one of America's most famous aviators. No one really knows for sure what happened to her after her plane disappeared.

The ships tried to contact the aviators, but there was no reply. They were missing.

The U.S. Navy and Coast Guard started searching for them right away. Searchers looked in the ocean and on surrounding islands. They found nothing. After a few weeks, they announced that the plane must have run out of fuel. It probably fell into the ocean. But no one could explain why no airplane parts or oil were found floating in the area.

Earhart's husband had other islands searched. After a time, he gave up, too. But others have continued the search.

Interesting Ideas

When someone is missing, people give many interesting ideas about what may have happened. Some people thought that Earhart and Noonan were spies for the U.S. government. They guessed that the Japanese rescued Earhart and Noonan, then kept them in a prison camp. There was even a movie made, based on that story.

Others say that Earhart gave up trying to fly around the world. But she was embarrassed. She and Noonan snuck back to the United States another way. People say that they changed their names and hid for the rest of their lives.

Another interesting story is still popular, although it has already been proven false. During World War II, Japanese radio stations had an American-sounding woman read the news. The woman would lie and say that Americans were losing the war. Her name was "Tokyo Rose." The rumor says that Earhart was forced to be "Tokyo Rose."

Still Searching...

Some people have made finding Amelia Earhart and her little plane a full-time job. They feel the need to know what happened to her. Every few years, someone finds a new clue. Or a scientist thinks of a new way to test one of the interesting ideas about Earhart's disappearance. TV shows act out her disappearance because people are so interested.

Almost 70 years later, experts might have found an explanation. A picture taken from the sky gave them an idea of where to look. The International Group for Historic Aircraft Recovery searched Nikumaroro Island in the Pacific Ocean. Nikumaroro is not too far from where Earhart's plane disappeared.

Found?

Searchers found parts of a plane and parts of a woman's shoe. Things found on Nikumaroro Island show that Earhart might have landed her plane on a coral reef around the island. Noonan might have died soon after landing. It seems that Earhart survived for several months.

The things found might be Earhart's and Noonan's. After several years of research, however, no one can prove that they were. Scientists think that a skeleton found on the island is Earhart's. But the skeleton has since been lost, so scientists cannot use new technology to prove it.

Is the mystery solved? We may never know for sure!

A stone in memory of Amelia Earhart stands in Burry Port, South Wales.

The Ninety-Nines

Ninety-nine women, including Amelia Earhart, started a pilot's club in 1929. The Ninety-Nines is a club for women aviators. Today, the club has more 6,000 members in countries all over the world.

The pilots meet to support each other in friendship, to learn more about aviation, and to race in friendly competitions. They also have mentor and scholarship programs to encourage new female flyers.

Besides being pilots, members do many other things. Some women work in fields other than aviation. Others are mechanics, air traffic controllers, and even astronauts. A few surviving original members are more than 80 years old, but they still fly to the meetings!

Earhart is not the only famous aviator from the club. Many members set world records. Several members trained pilots for World War II.

Bessie Coleman was the world's first African American female pilot. She died in 1926, before the Ninety-Nines was founded. But she has been honored by the club. Another member, Colonel Pamela Melroy, is not only a pilot with the U.S. Air Force, but she is also an astronaut with NASA.

Twins Reunite
DATAFILE

TIMELINE

November 1982
Twin girls, Adriana and Tamara, are born in Mexico. Each girl is adopted by a different U.S. family.

November 2002
The girls meet for the first time.

Where is Mexico?

KEY TERMS

adopt - to take someone into your family and raise the person as if he or she were your own

identical - two things looking so similar that they are essentially the same

identical twins - the result of an egg that splits into two halves that develop into two babies

fraternal twins - the result of two eggs released at the same time that develop into two babies

rabbi - a Jewish religious leader

DID YOU KNOW?

Twins can be fraternal or identical. Although identical twins always look alike, fraternal twins often look different. Twin births make up less than three percent of all births in the United States.

Chapter Three:
Twins Reunite

Have you ever been told you look just like someone else? Two girls heard this so often, they decided to check out the story. When they met, they said it was like looking in a mirror. That day they learned that they were not only sisters—they were also identical twins!

Up for Adoption

Late in 1982, the Scotts flew to Mexico to adopt a baby girl. She had just been born. The Scotts wanted to raise the baby girl as if she were their own daughter. They would call her Adriana.

When the Scotts got to Mexico, they learned that their new baby had an identical twin sister. Identical twins are children born at the same time. When the girls were born, one baby needed more care. This baby was Adriana. But the girls' birth mother had disappeared with the other baby.

Soon the Scott family took Adriana home to New York. The Scotts tried to find the other baby. All they were told was that a rabbi, a Jewish religious leader, and his family had adopted her. Since they could not find her sister, the Scotts decided never to tell Adriana that she had a twin.

Little did they know that Tamara, the twin sister, was close by. Tamara also lived in New York, within 25 miles of the Scotts. Tamara was not adopted by a rabbi, but a family whose name was Rabi. The Rabis were never told that their daughter was a twin. They never knew to look for Tamara's sister.

A Pushy Guest

When Tamara turned 20, she had a party with her college friends. One friend brought Justin to the party. Justin could not stop staring at Tamara when he first met her.

"You look exactly like Adriana, this girl I'm seeing…" Justin told Tamara. Tamara had been told before that she had a familiar face. But as Tamara started eating her cake, Justin would not leave her alone. He told her, "she was born in Mexico."

"So was I," said Tamara.

"Well," said Justin, "she was adopted from Mexico."

"So was I!" said Tamara.

Then Justin told her that his girlfriend, Adriana, had also just turned 20. Tamara decided to find out about this other girl. Justin called Adriana to ask if he could give Tamara her e-mail address. Soon the girls were talking online.

The Twins Meet

Adriana told her mother about Tamara. Mrs. Scott asked Adriana to ask Tamara for her last name. When the answer came back as Rabi, Mrs. Scott knew Adriana's twin had found them.

She then told Adriana everything. Adriana was so excited. She wrote back to Tamara that they were twins. When Adriana sent a picture of herself, Tamara knew she had to believe her.

Soon the girls decided to meet. The twins were very nervous about meeting each other. One girl got so nervous, she almost cancelled. But soon the twins finally met.

One girl said, "I'm looking at me." They were even wearing the same jacket. They discovered that they had much more in common.

During their first meeting, neither girl looked at her sister much. They were both still so shocked to find out about each other. It was a good thing their friends kept them talking!

Meeting the Parents

Tamara brought Adriana to meet her adoptive mother. Mrs. Rabi did not believe that Tamara had a twin. She did not, that is, until Adriana walked in the door with her daughter. The way they looked, walked, and even talked was enough to convince anyone.

Tamara's mother was very sad at first. She was afraid Tamara would not think of her as family anymore. Tamara told her adoptive mother that she would always love Mrs. Rabi as her mother. In fact, she said that her mom should know that she has a new daughter in her twin sister.

Another Meeting

Adriana and Tamara were very happy to each have a sister. They told everyone about the strange way they found out about each other.

Soon people at a television station heard the twins' story. They wanted to do a show about the girls. The station flew the girls and their adoptive mothers to Mexico. The station hired a detective to find the twins' mother, Norma de la Cruz. Norma actually lived in California. So the station flew Norma to meet her daughters in Mexico. Norma was able to answer many questions the twins had for her.

Today, Tamara and Adriana still enjoy getting to know each other as sisters. They also keep in touch with their birth mother. The twins enjoy getting together. They consider each other a sister and a friend. What a wonderful present to get for your twentieth birthday—a twin sister!

Reunited twins, Adriana and Tamara, are still getting to know one another.

The Science of Twins

Identical twins are born when an egg splits as it forms. The egg usually splits very early in a woman's pregnancy.

If an egg splits after the first few days, the egg may start to split, but is less likely to finish. When this happens, the babies stay physically joined. This is known as conjoined twins, or Siamese twins.

In the years 1980 to 1997, twin births increased by 42 percent, from 19 twin births to 27 twin births in 1,000 births. This made up 2.7 percent of all births in the United States.

Identical Twins

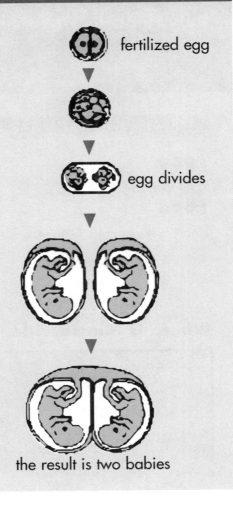

fertilized egg

egg divides

the result is two babies

TIMELINE

1969
RFID tags are invented.
1996
Universal pet chip scanners are first used.

Where is Martinsville, IN?

KEY TERMS

RFID - Radio Frequency Identification Device

implant - to permanently place an object inside the body

database - a list of related information, such as a phone book

encode - using a code to store information

DID YOU KNOW?

Vets can implant an identification chip under the skin in the back of a pet's neck. To keep the chip from moving to a different part of the pet's body, the chip has a special coating. This coating helps the chip bond with the tissue in the pet's body.

Chapter Four:
Tuffy Finds His Way Home

Anna Cox lives in Martinsville, Indiana. Back in the year 2000, she put her dog, Tuffy, in the backyard and chained him up, so he could not run away. Tuffy is a black-and-brown six-year-old Lhasa Apso mix. Lhasa Apsos are small dogs with long hair that can cover their eyes. Earlier, Anna had a tiny electronic dog tag, about the size of a grain of rice, implanted under Tuffy's skin. It was a good thing she did.

Tuffy Gets Free

The next time Anna Cox looked in her backyard, only the chain and collar remained. Tuffy was gone. He had wiggled out of his collar and disappeared. It would be a long time before Anna Cox would see Tuffy again.

Three years later, a woman named Sherry Baumann drove to work in Indianapolis. Indianapolis, the capitol of Indiana, is 32 miles away from from Martinsville. As Sherry Baumann drove, she spotted a small dog trotting along the busy road.

A Good Samaritan

Sherry Baumann, who has four dogs of her own, was worried the little dog might get hit by a car. So she pulled over, called to the dog, and waived a biscuit. Happy, but dirty and hungry, the dog came to Sherry Baumann. The dog had no collar or anything visible to identify it. Sherry Baumann put the dog in her van and drove to the Animal Care and Control Center.

Workers at the center pulled out a small handheld device. It was a scanner. It could detect special electronic tags that are sometimes inserted under a pet's skin. As the workers waved the scanner over the stray dog, a number popped up on the scanner. The dog, it turned out, had been tagged. Radio waves from the scanner activated the tag from under the dog's skin.

RFIDs Save the Day

When the workers looked up the tag number in a database, they discovered the dog's name was Tuffy. They called Anna Cox and told her about her long-lost dog. Imagine how surprised she was to receive such a phone call! Anna Cox and Tuffy were reunited after three long years apart.

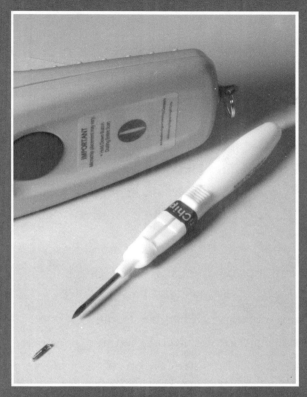

An RFID device, like the one Anna Cox had implanted in her dog, Tuffy

RFIDs: Bar Codes of the Future

Tuffy is a small dog. But his story is connected with the largest retailer in the world, Wal-Mart. In 1984, Wal-Mart decided it wanted a better way to track items coming into and out of its stores. So the company asked its suppliers to put bar codes on all of their products.

Twenty years later, Wal-Mart is again pushing for an easier way to track its goods: RFID tags are the answer. These tiny devices are like electronic bar codes. But instead of someone scanning the products, the tags can be read wirelessly by a scanner.

The tags are encoded with a long number. That number is linked in a database to information about the product. A scanner reads the tag's code and looks up the information in a database, all in an instant.

These tags have existed for 35 years. Until recently, they have been too big and too expensive to be used widely. But for at least a decade, they have been used to track lost pets. Vets inject the tag under the pet's skin. Then if the pet gets lost, the tag can be scanned, and the code can reveal who the pet's owner is and where the pet lives.

Some people say such tags could be injected into people. With RFID tags, people would not need to stand in line to pay groceries. They could just walk out and let a scanner detect the information about all of the purchases and the person shopping. But others say tagging people would invade privacy and the information could be abused. What do you think?

The HMS *Beagle* is Found

DATAFILE

1817

The HMS *Beagle* is built.

February 2004

The remains of the *Beagle* are found in mud in an abandoned port in England

Where is England?

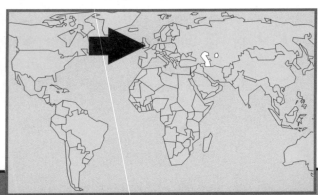

KEY TERMS

evolution - the development within a group of living things

historical documents - anything written in the past

radar - the way of using radio waves to find distant objects

replica - a copy of an original object or piece of art

DID YOU KNOW?

A tortoise that Charles Darwin took from its home on his famous trip is the oldest known living animal on Earth. Her name is Harriet. She was born on the Galapagos Islands. She is thought to be more than 170 years old. Harriet now lives in a zoo in Australia.

Chapter Five:
The HMS *Beagle* is Found

The *Beagle* was not a dog. Nor did it actually belong to scientist Charles Darwin. But the ship that Darwin lived on for five years helped him in his work. In fact, Darwin said that the trip was "the most important event in my life."

The *Beagle*

The ship was built to be part of the British navy. It had cannons and was built to guard the coast. After a few years, the cannons were taken off the boat. The *Beagle* was then used for scientific explorations. At one point, Captain FitzRoy asked Charles Darwin to come aboard as his science officer.

The Famous Trip

When the *Beagle* left port in 1831, Darwin felt so seasick he almost asked the captain to turn around. But by the end of the trip, Darwin was glad he stayed.

The five-year-long trip took Darwin all over the world. He explored places and took lots of notes. He even collected plants and animals from these new places.

After careful study of his collection and notes, Darwin came up with a new idea—a very new idea—about how living things developed. Scientists today still base their work on Darwin's ideas. People all over the world still debate his idea of evolution.

What Happened After

After his trip, Darwin presented his ideas to other scientists. The *Beagle* continued sailing. After a while, the British navy again used it to guard the coastline.

In 1870, the navy retired the 50-year-old boat. They sold the wooden ship for parts. No one kept records of where the ship went after that. The HMS *Beagle* was lost.

The Recovery

Soon the story of Darwin's trip aboard the HMS *Beagle* became famous. Curious modern scientists wondered what happened to the ship.

In 2002, scientists formed a group called the *Beagle* Ship Research Group. The scientists started playing detective. They looked at historical documents.

They found records of the ship's sale. The group used old maps to see where the HMS *Beagle* had been docked.

The scientists found the dock. An old anchor was stuck in the mud. They used a new kind of radar to see what was underground. The radar showed that a boat was buried in more than 10 feet of mud. It was the same size as the HMS *Beagle*. But the radar showed that parts of the ship were missing. Besides that, the ship in the mud was the same shape as the HMS *Beagle*.

As of 2004, the group still needed money to uncover the ship. Only then could they be sure that it actually is the HMS *Beagle*. The scientists wonder if the ship still contains anything from Darwin's trip. They hope to be able to find out someday soon!

Even if the boat is uncovered, it is no longer complete. A group of people interested in history formed their own club called The *Beagle* Project.

The club is building a replica of the famous boat. A replica is a copy of an original. The club dresses up in clothes like those Darwin and Captain FitzRoy would have worn. This club will help others learn about the HMS *Beagle* and her famous crew.

Beagle 2

One of the 2003 spacecraft journeying to Mars was named *Beagle 2*, after Darwin's famed ship. British professor and scientist, Colin Pillinger, was involved with both the spacecraft and the discovery of the original sea-going ship. In fact, he was the one to name the spaceship.

Sadly, the *Beagle 2* has become another mystery. Scientists lost contact with it and cannot tell what happened. Maybe they should look in the mud on Mars!

Book Review

If you enjoyed learning about Amelia Earhart, read more about her in this book: *Amelia Earhart: First Lady of Flight* by Jan Parr. New York: Franklin Watts, 1997.

This book describes Earhart's life. Reading about the pilot's early life is interesting and sometimes surprising. For example, the first plane Earhart saw did not interest her at all. In fact, until she did fall in love with flying, Earhart wanted to work in a hospital!

Amelia Earhart also had faults and made many mistakes. This book describes both the good and the bad, which makes Earhart seem more like a real person. Described in more detail is Earhart's disappearance and last known locations.

Amelia Earhart: First Lady of Flight contains many pictures of Earhart and others she knew. At the end of the book, you can find a list of the records Earhart set. Also, a timeline lists easy-to-read facts and dates about important parts of Earhart's life. It is like an at-a-glance summary of her life.

There are many more books to read about Amelia Earhart, and this book lists some of them. There is also a list of suggested movies and websites. Finally, what makes *Amelia Earhart: First Lady of Flight* really interesting is that the director of the Ninety-Nines helped the author find the facts.

Glossary

adopt: to take someone into your family and raise the person as if he or she were your own

amphitheater: an open, oval arena with seats around it

artifact: a man-made object from a period in the past

aviation: the science of flying an aircraft

C.E.: Common Era; the years from 1 to the present

database: a list of related information, such as a phone book

encode: using a code to store information

equator: an imaginary line at the widest place around Earth

erupt: to explode violently

evolution: the development within a group of living things

fraternal twins: the result of two eggs released at the same time that develop into two babies

historical documents: anything written in the past

Thinking It Over

1. What does it feel like
   to do something really well?

2. What is something
   you have done
   that was good enough to sign?

3. What does it take
   to work out a problem
   between two people?

identical: two things looking so similar that they are essentially the same

identical twins: the result of an egg that splits into two halves that develop into two babies

implant: to permanently place an object inside the body

Mount Vesuvius: a volcano in Italy that has been active for centuries

navigator: one who plans the path of a ship or aircraft

pioneer: a person who opens up new areas of land, thought, or technology

rabbi: a Jewish religious leader

radar: the way of using radio waves to find distant objects

replica: a copy of an original object or piece of art

RFID: Radio Frequency Identification Device

Index